The Brokenness Words

Leave Behind

by

Blake Newsom

I Hope this finds you well.
—Blake Newsom.

Cover artwork done by
Elizabeth Fisher

THE AMERICAN

SUICIDE & CRISIS LIFELINE

THE WORLDWIDE SUICIDE LIFELINE

Artist Recognition

The artwork for this book would not be possible without the help of Ms. Struab who is one of the art teachers at Shelbyville Central High School located in Shelbyville, Tennessee. The artwork was done by her students, who are very talented artists.

Jenny Saldierna
lxxxiii
Jacari Whitaker
lxv
Kevin Lopez
lxxxvii
Payton Rupprecht
lv
Hugo Leandro Juan
lxi
Oren Taylor
xliv
Olivia Anderson
xxxvii, xlii
Kara Ruth
xiv, xxxv, xxxix

Rosalia Viveros
xxviii
Alexa Barrera
ix
Aidan Flores
xci
Elizabeth Fisher
xxxi, xlv, xlix, xcv, xc
Kaylee Smith
xvii, lxxxv
Michaela Wilhoite xlv, lvi
Claire King
liii, lxvii, lxxvii
Selena Bartolome
xxxi

Gabriella Luna Lona
xxxvi, xlviii
Martin Mateo
lix

Janet Hernandez
xxiii, lxix, lxxiii, lxiii
Amani Cummings
xxvii

Zoe Rodriguez
lxxxi
Joanna Chen
lxxv

Michelle Santiago Vitervo
xli
Disha Patel
xxxiii
Carolina Francisco
xxv

Evelyn Morales
xxvi
Alejandro Contreras Cabrera
xxxviii, li

Denise Gonzalez
xxi, lii
Kenzie Carter
lvii, lxxi, lxxix

Lilly Grey
lii
Rocio Cruces
xix
Cora Capers
xiii
Gael Lozano
xi

Table of Contents

A

Child Broken by Society viii

Trauma x

Shout out to my Bullies xii

Strong Enough xiv

Their Words Stay xvi

The Forest xviii

A

Message to The Suicidal xx

Stepdad xxii

The Last Time xxiv

Change xxvi

Addicted to Knowledge xxviii

Happiness xxx

Light and Darkness xxxii

Choice xxxiv

Healing xxxvi

Slaves to Time xxxviii

People Stare xl

Beauty From Ashes xlii

Wildfire xliv

For Now xlvi

Yahweh xlviii

Revenge l

Looking Back lii

Different liv

Destiny lvi

Thoughts lviii

A
Child Broken by Society

Why am I like this?

What did I do to deserve

this kind of treatment?

Why are they so mean to me,

I'm so nice to them.

After a while you get used to

their hurtful words.

It still hurts, nonetheless.

Why did my teachers not say anything to my classmates

bullying me.

I know they heard what they said to me.

Am I not worth defending,

is what they said

true.

Why do they laugh

at the pain they

cause me.

People tell me it's

because they're

hurting.

But that's no

excuse to treat

people this way.

Don't they see, I'm

hurting too?

Yet, I choose

kindness.

Trauma

Trauma,

the thing that keeps everyone up at night.

Thinking, trying to understand.

Why people say,

"That's not real trauma."

Trauma comes in

all shapes and sizes.

Shout out to my Bullies

From the bullies in school, to the bullies

at church, to even the bullies in my own family.

You taught me early on

how the world was going to treat me.

SHOUT OUT TO MY BULLIES!

You showed me the world is not a fair place.

No one will stand up for ME except ME.

SHOUT OUT TO MY BULLIES!

You helped create

the type of person who will change the world.

SHOUT OUT TO MY BULLIES!

Strong Enough

I was strong enough then,

I'm strong enough now,

I will always be strong enough.

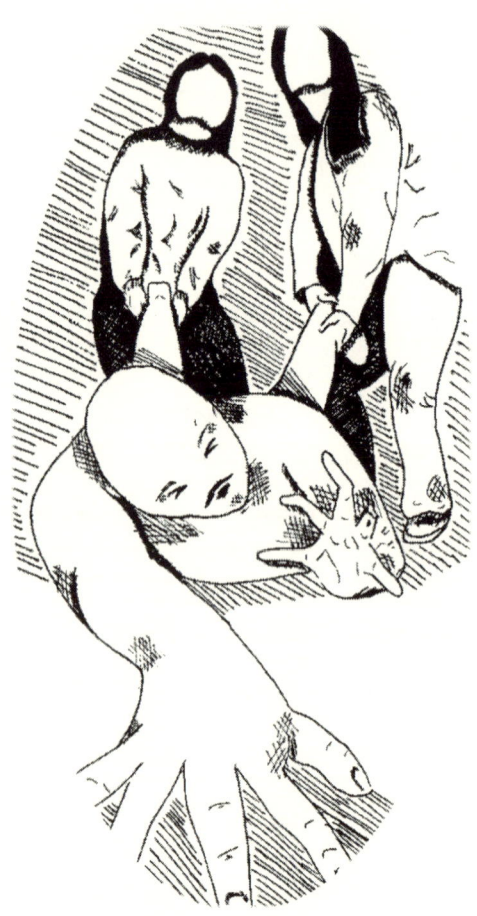

Their Words Stay

Many young adults go

out and have fun at the bars and the clubs.

But I, well I stay home or

in the forest.

Why you ask?

I'm still healing,

healing from words of my past.

I'm safe at home.

Some people

are scared of the forest and

the monsters that lurk in them.

If you ask me,

the people of this world are the true monsters.

xvii

The Forest

I've never felt more

alive then when

I'm in the Forest.

The way the wind blows,

ever so gracefully.

That it

sounds as if the tree is

an old guitar and the leaves are the strings.

They play such a beautiful melody

and

in that moment,

I find peace with the world.

A
Message to The Suicidal

Don't do it.

I write this to you from

A boy who once was full of depression, to now a grown

man who Loves life down to the very last detail.

I have learned there is nothing

time cannot fix.

When you feel depressed say:

I AM WORTH IT.

THINGS WILL GET BETTER.

LIFE IS WORTH IT.

I AM LOVED.

I AM STRONG ENOUGH.

I CHOOSE LIFE!

xxi

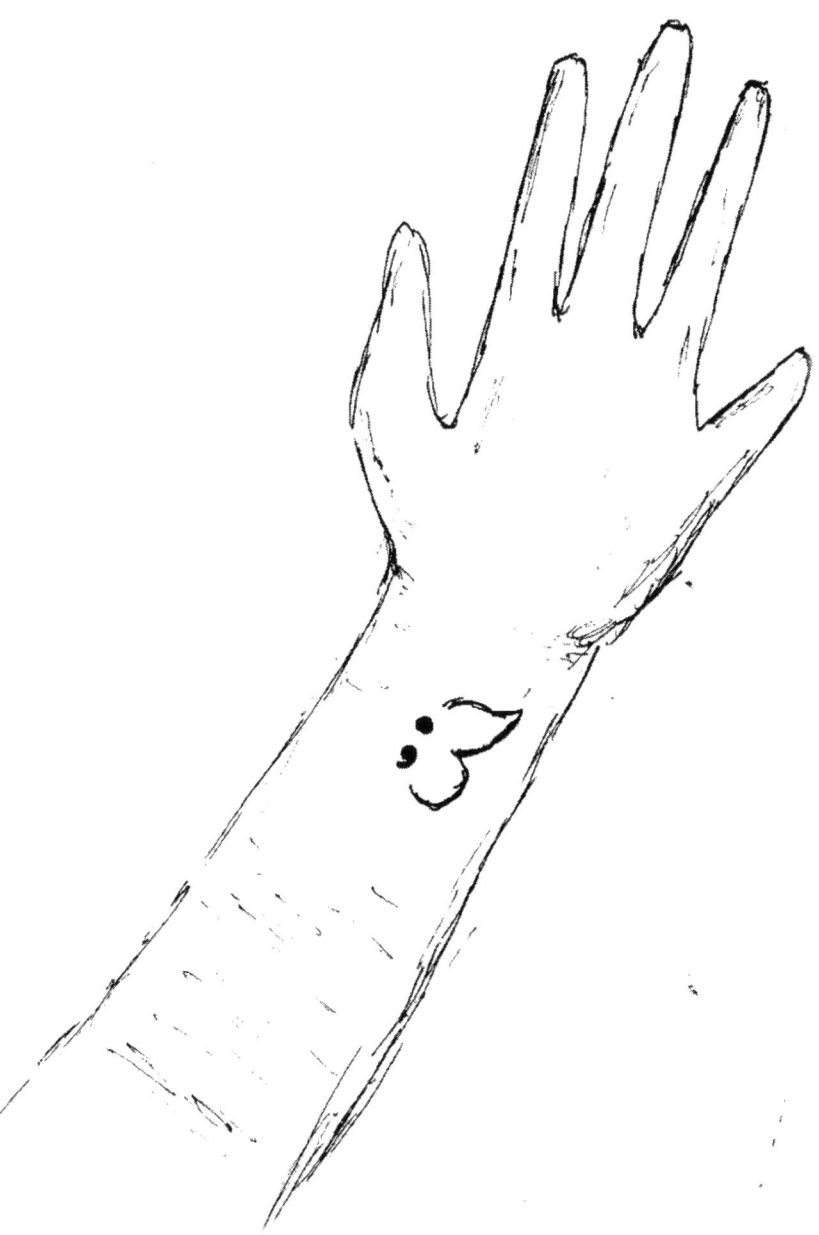

Stepdad

What is a stepdad?

Everyone's definition is different. But here is my definition,

A man who teaches his children that family isn't blood.

A stepdad teaches his children what family means.

Family is the people who love and care for you and are there for you when you need them.

The people who can make you angrier than you thought possible. Then five minutes later you're laughing making more memories with them.

A man who shows what unconditional love looks like.

A stepdad is man who changes your life forever.

xxiii

The Last Time

This is the last time.

I'm nobodies second Choice.

I know my worth.

If they don't see my worth.

They'll lose me.

Now I'm all alone.

But at least I have

peace and happiness.

I am enough.

XXV

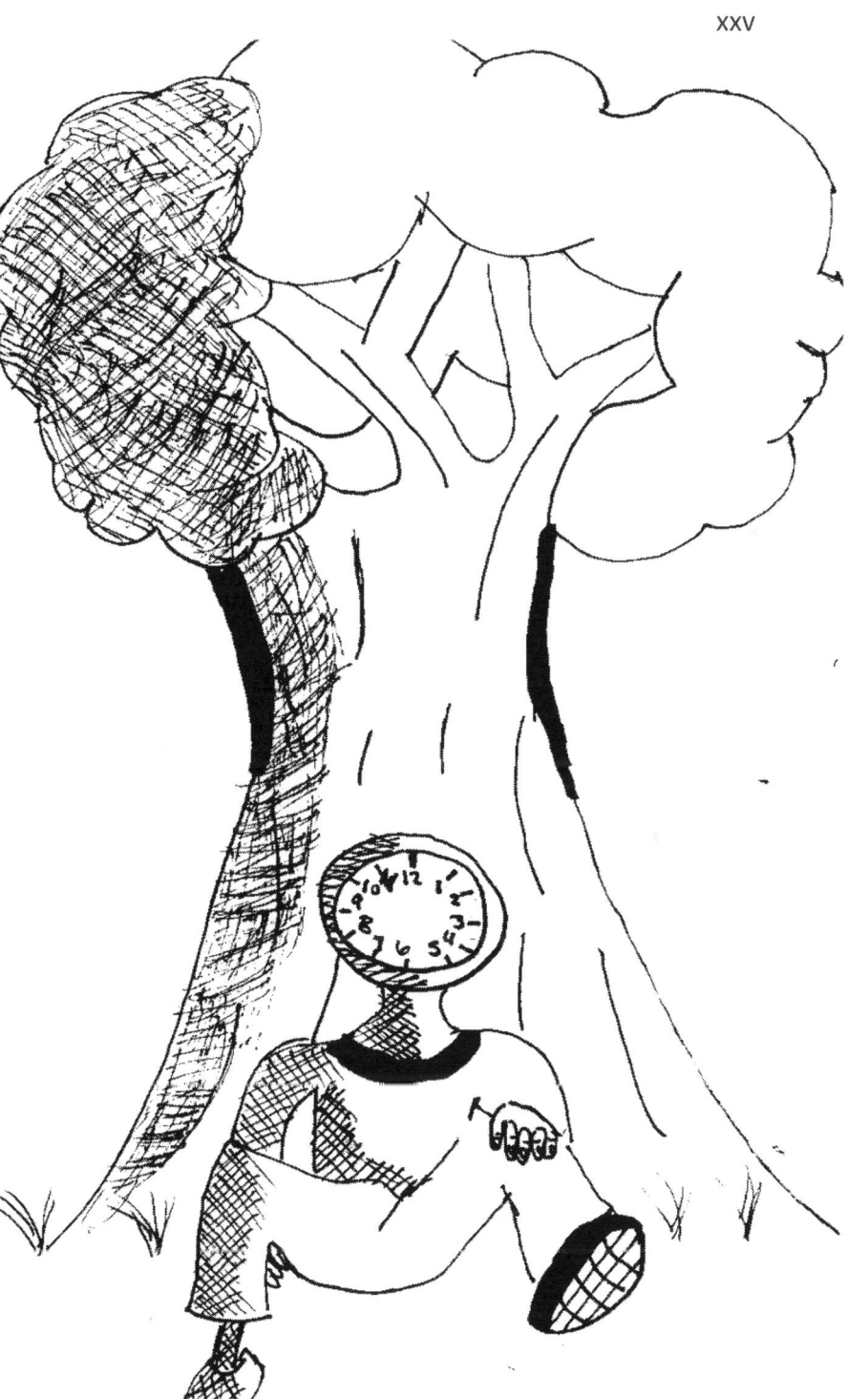

Change

Without the desire to change,

one will never get better.

Once you crave change,

it'll change your life forever.

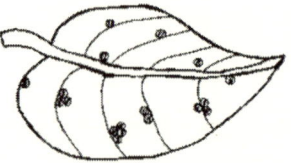

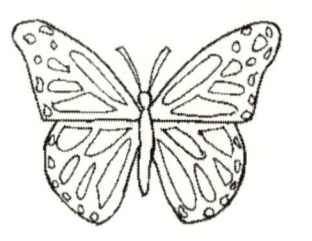
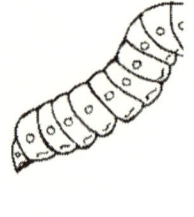

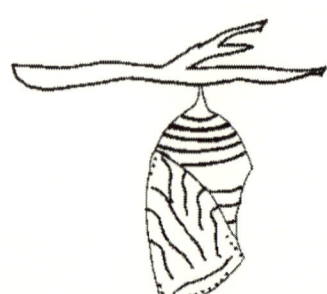

Addicted to Knowledge

Some are addicted to

drugs or alcohol.

My addiction is the

desire to understand mankind.

It's both a blessing and a curse.

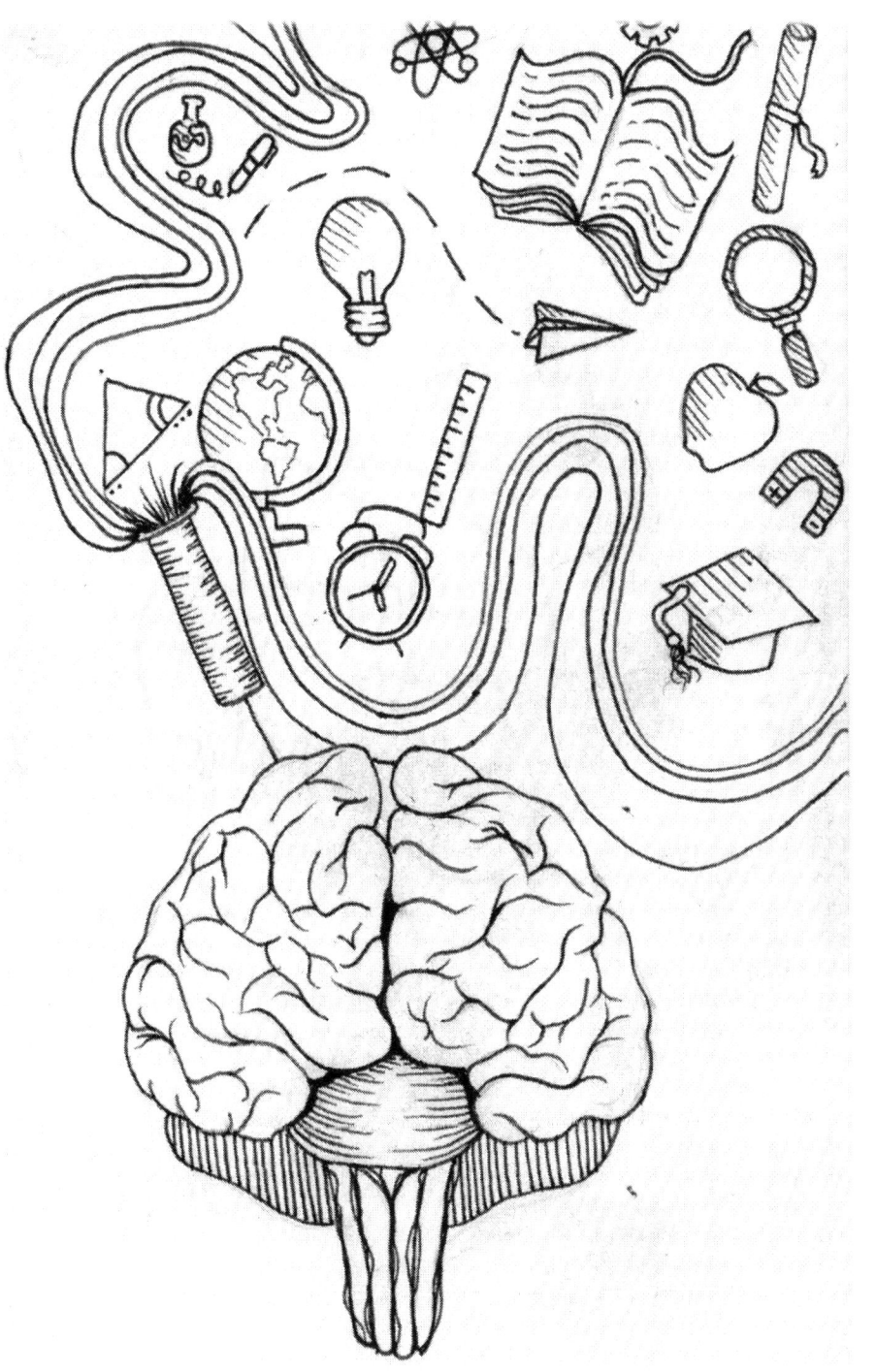

Happiness

I find happiness in

the moment.

I find happiness in seeing a

society thrive.

I find happiness in watching

the river flow and the wind blow.

I find happiness in the

laughter of others.

I find happiness in the

meaningless conversations,

the ones that mean everything.

I have found happiness.

Light and Darkness

Produce nothing but light

and

only light will surround you.

Produce darkness

and

darkness will surround you like

the dark of night surrounds the moon.

Choice

Everyone has a choice,

to be good or to be bad,

to be the hero or to be a villain.

The choice is yours to make

and yours alone.

Healing

Forgive,

don't do it for them.

Do it for yourself.

Revenge doesn't heal,

forgive everyone.

xxxvii

Slaves to Time

We are all slaves to time.

Time knows all and takes all.

Time, the one thing we never get back.

Time, don't waste it, enjoy it.

One day you will have no time left.

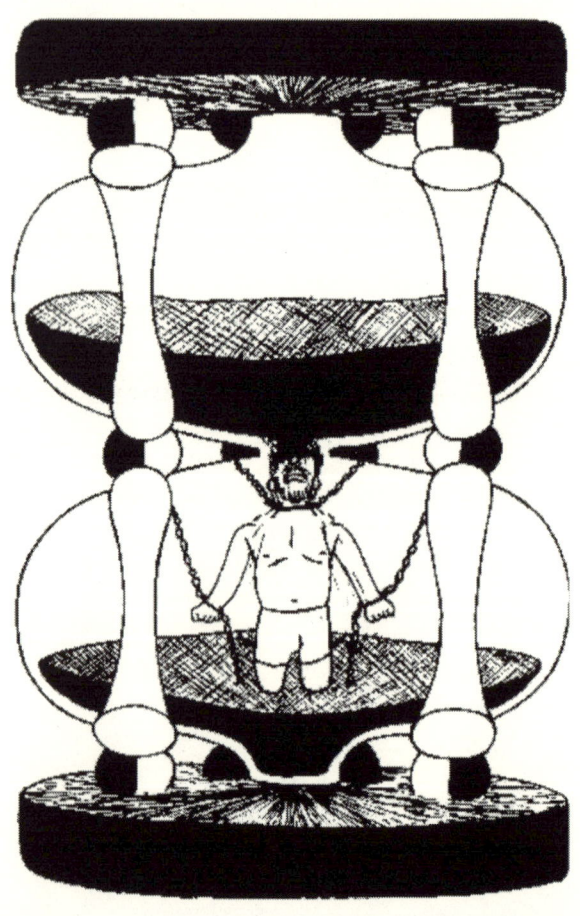

People Stare

People stare,

everywhere I go.

I used to hate their

glaring eyes.

Why do they stare,

I would like to know.

But now I enjoy it.

Stare on

my darlings.

Beauty From Ashes

I look back on all the times

I was broken with words, by the mundanes of this

world.

I see now what Yahweh

Meant, when he said

I will paint beauty from your

ashes.

xliii

Wildfire

I was once just a dim light in this world.

Now I'm a wildfire, going after anything and everything I want.

I will not stop until I have it all.

xlv

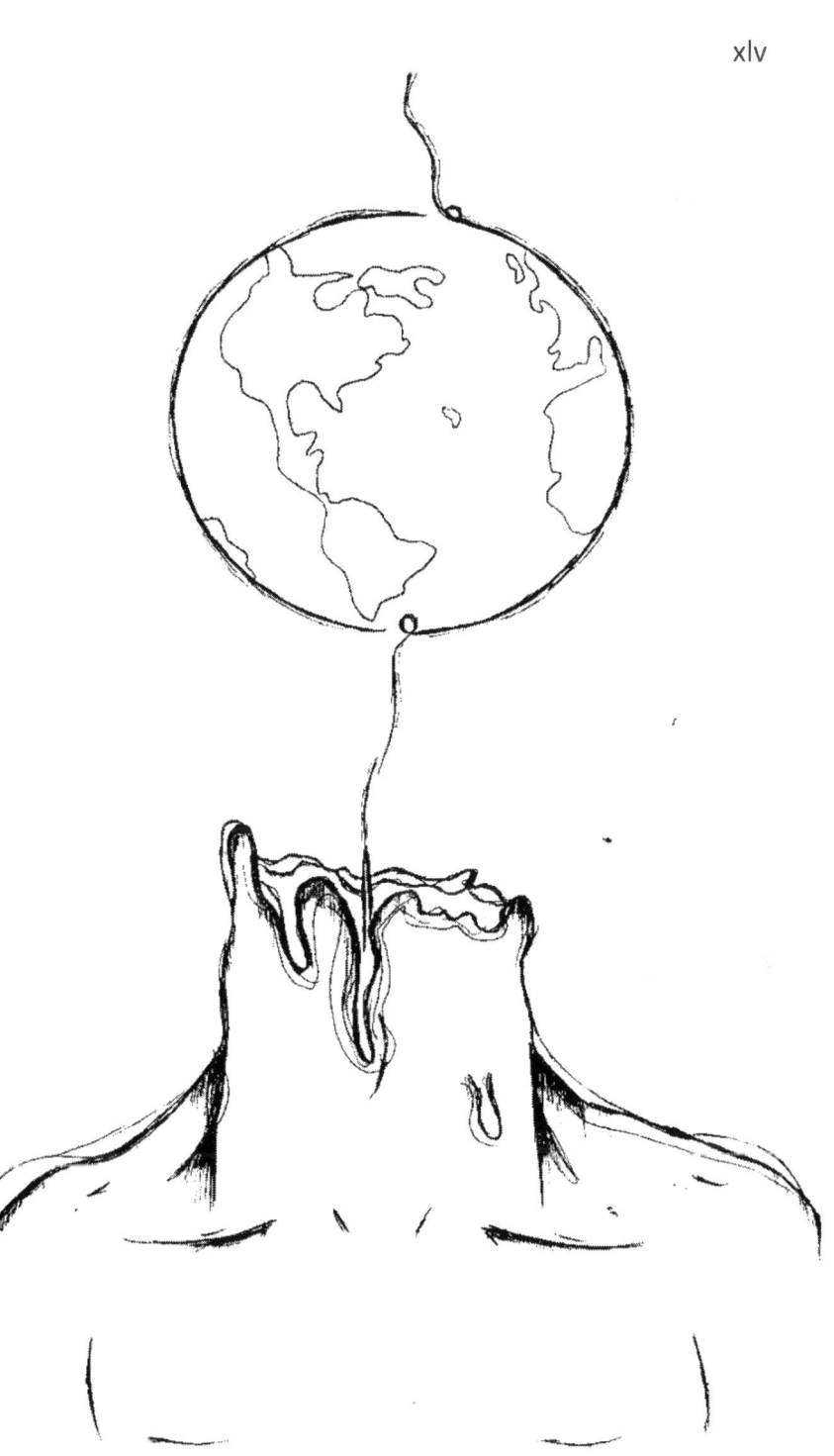

For Now

For now, I am

kind.

For now, I am

caring.

For now, I am

compassion.

For now, I am

loving.

For now, I am

outgoing.

For now,

I never settle for less.

For now, I am

supercalifragilisticexpialidocious.

xlvii

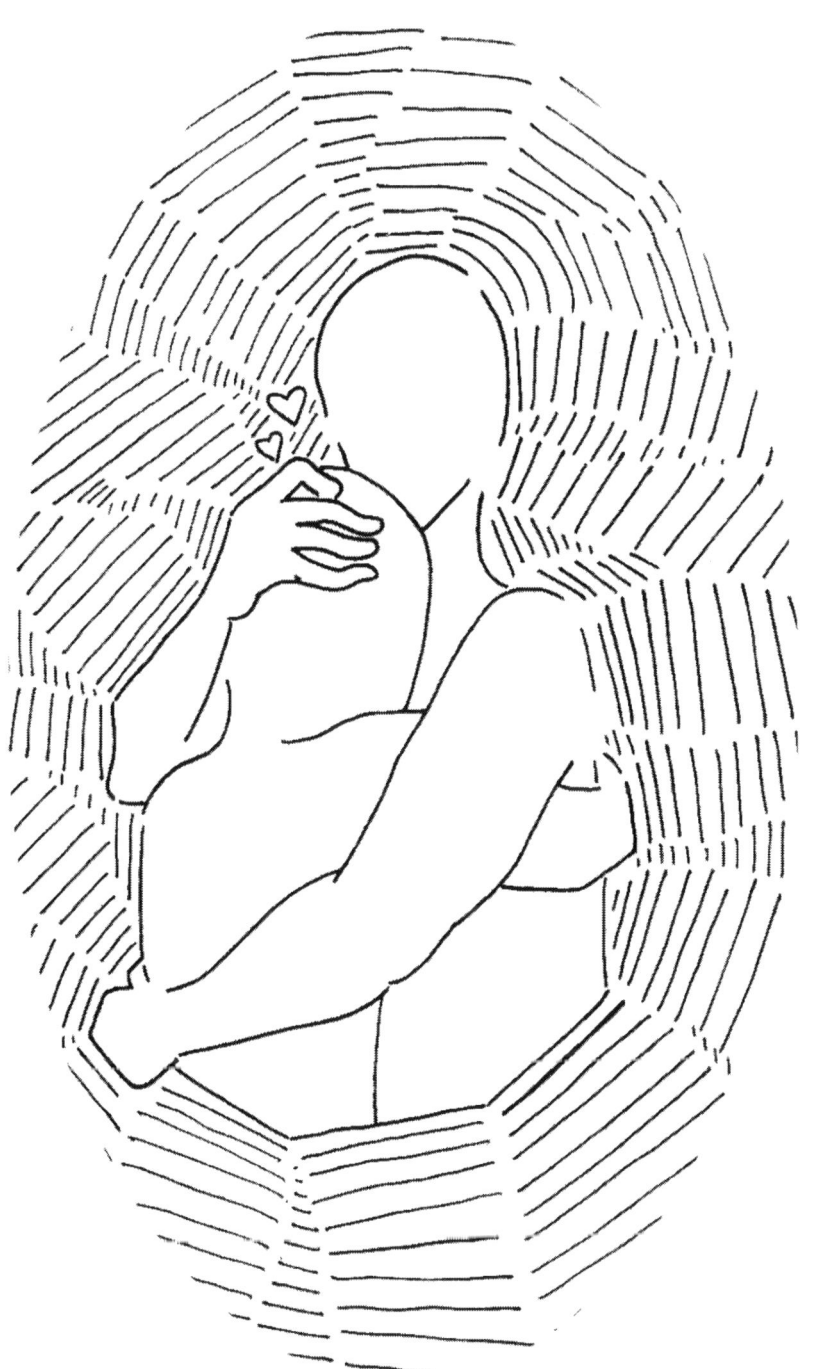

Yahweh

Yahweh's heart breaks for the people who turn from

him because of his followers.

Yahweh, he sees

And

knows everything.

All Yahweh has ever wanted

was to love you,

for you

and

nothing less

of

YOU.

xlix

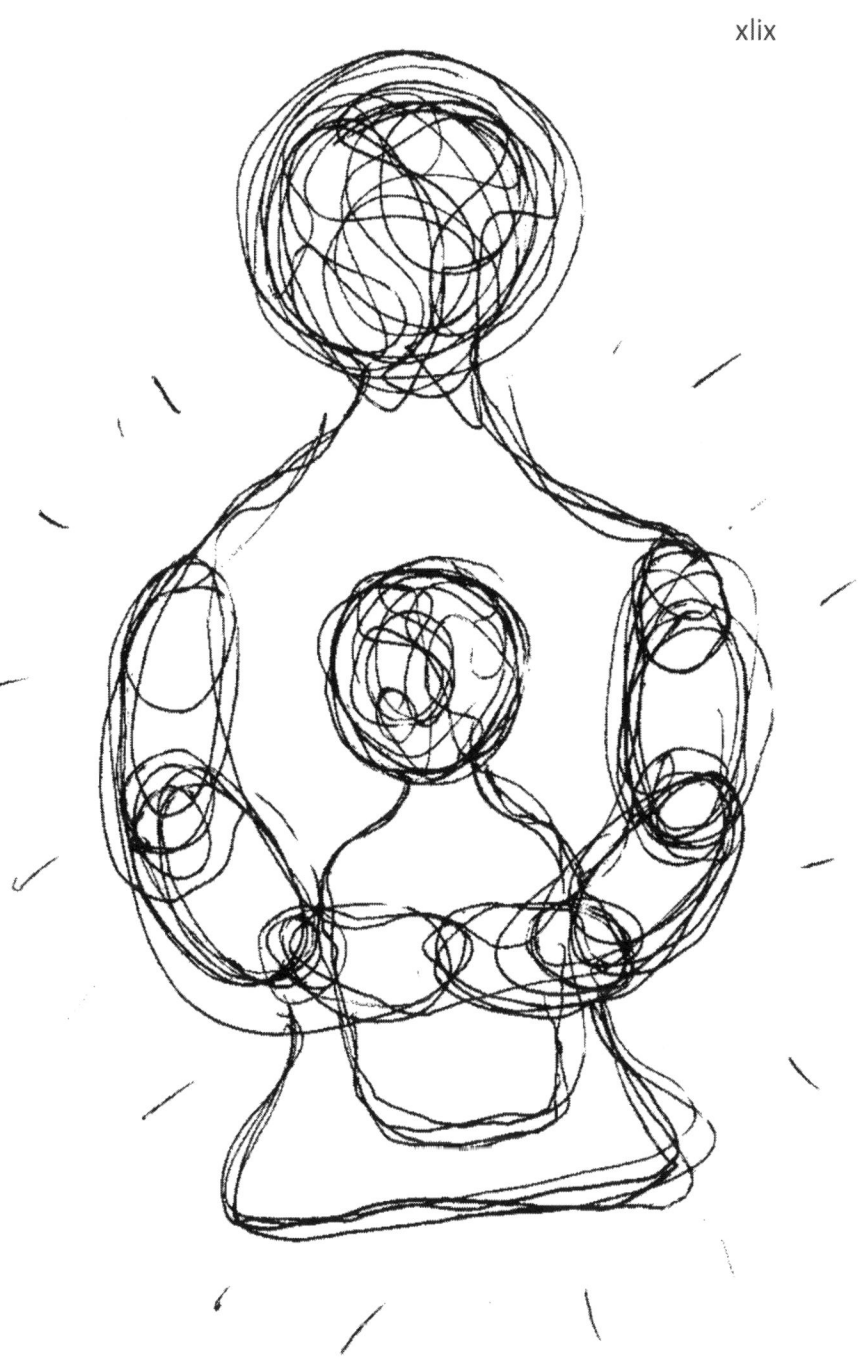

Revenge

Revenge,

It's not mine,

and it's not yours.

Revenge belongs to

one and one alone.

All who have caused pain,

will feel pain.

For God and the universe,

demand balance.

Looking Back

I can look back and see their faces.

But,

their words will not be heard,

and

the Pain will not be felt.

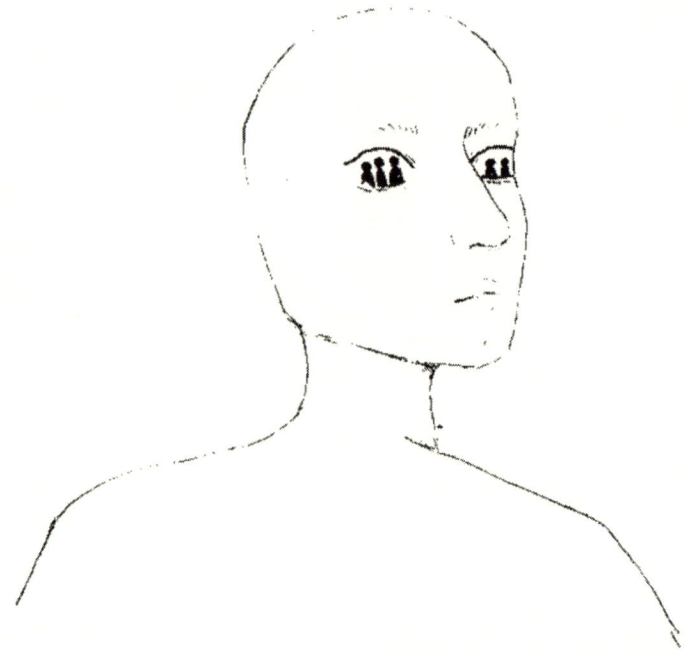

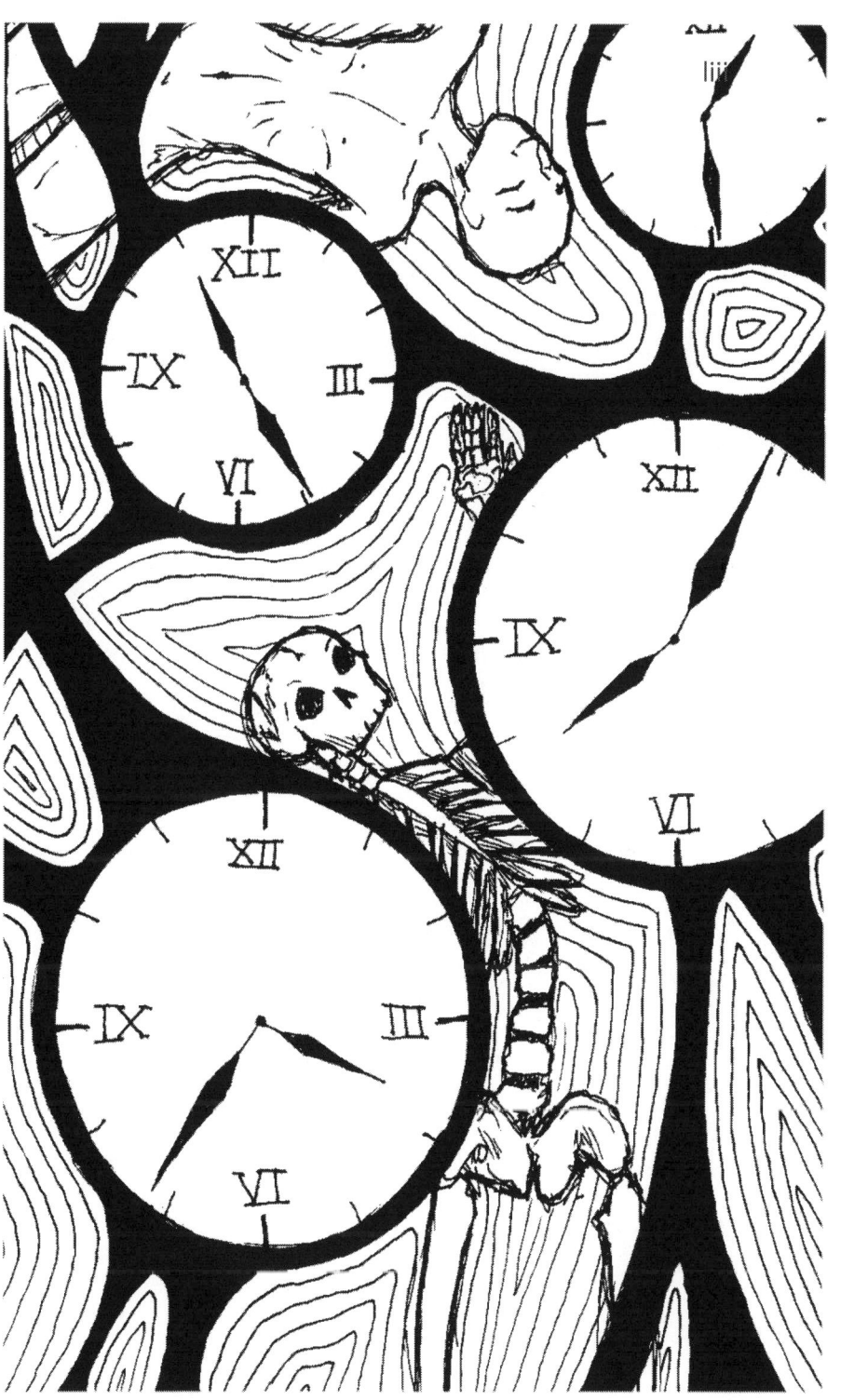

Different

The ones who are bullied for being different.

Those are the same ones who change the world,

simply because they're different.

Destiny

For your destiny,

was written in stone eons before you were even

thought about on this earth.

You're destined for greatness.

Thoughts

These are my thoughts.

Will they make any sense,

who knows?

I'm sure you'll be the judge of that,

enjoy.

Sometimes I feel nothing.

Not excited.

Not happy.

Not sad.

Just

Nothing.

I just wish I knew why?

You're perfect.

You're loved.

The world is so much better when you're in it,

spreading joy and laughter.

lxiii

Happiness is a choice,

without the desire to change.

You'll never be happy.

You simply

won't.

lxv

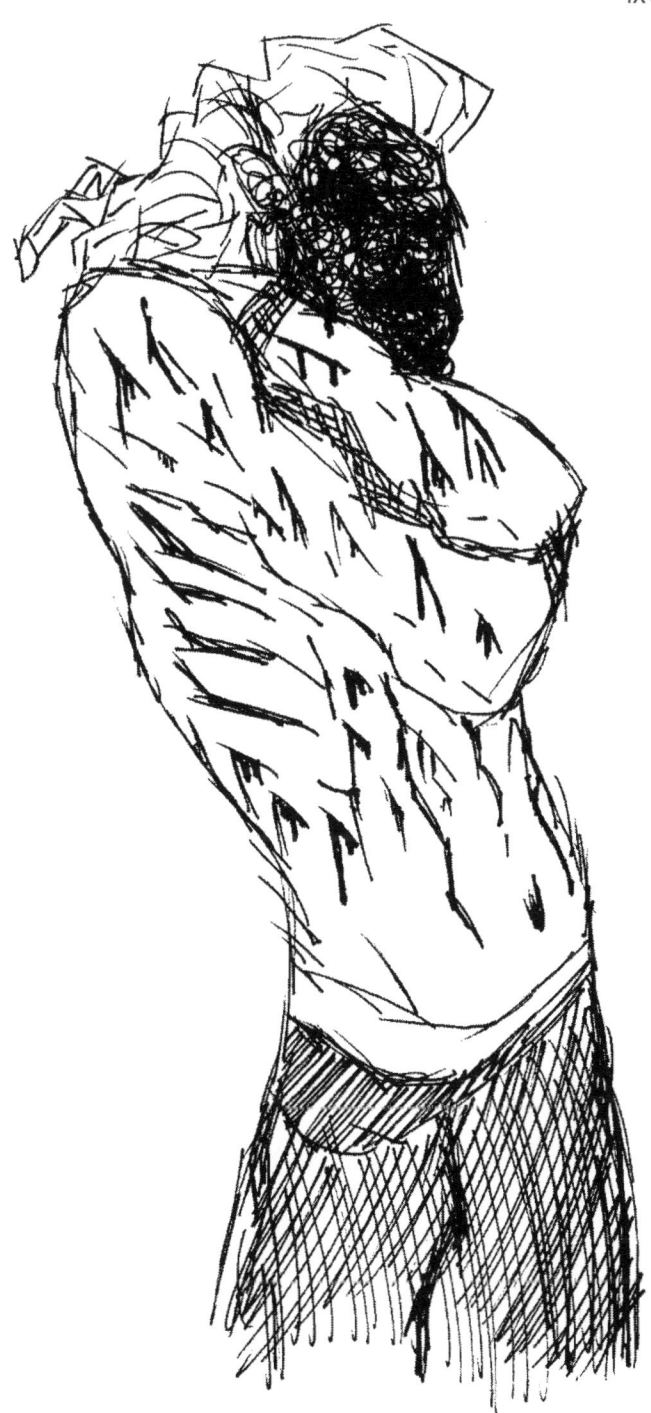

What makes other people normal,

But not I.

I want anything but normal.

I want adventure and excitement.

I want to go everywhere

and

see everything.

Isn't that normal?

Do not let your story be

written by someone else.

Take back control of your narrative.

You are the writer for your story.

So, make it extraordinary, you won't get a second

chance.

lxix

If you cannot find a way out,

make a way out.

Be the light the world

needs on the darkest of nights.

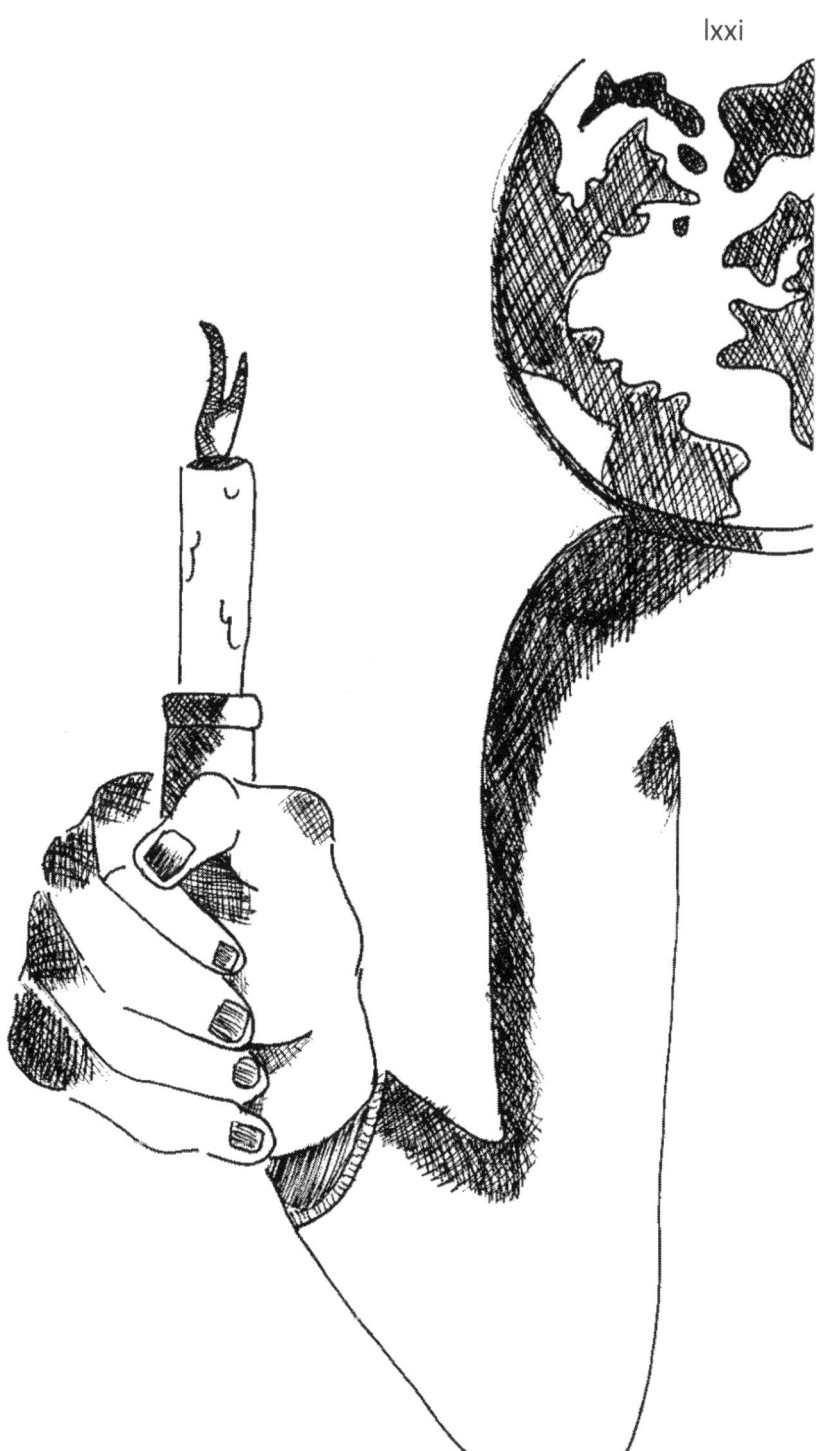

I cannot help but to weep in sorrow,

when I hear and see the pain that people cause.

Surely not everyone

enjoys the suffering of others.

Surely there is still

some good left in the world.

I know there is good left in the world,

I'm in it.

Where are the other people like me?

lxxiii

I wish people truly understood the power of words.

During my short few years in this world, I have learned prayer and manifestation are two of the realest things I have ever witness.

I have prayed and spoken things that have come to past too many times for it to be a coincidence.

Watch what you

say and sing.

When anyone speaks, they're manifesting.

God is always listening.

lxxv

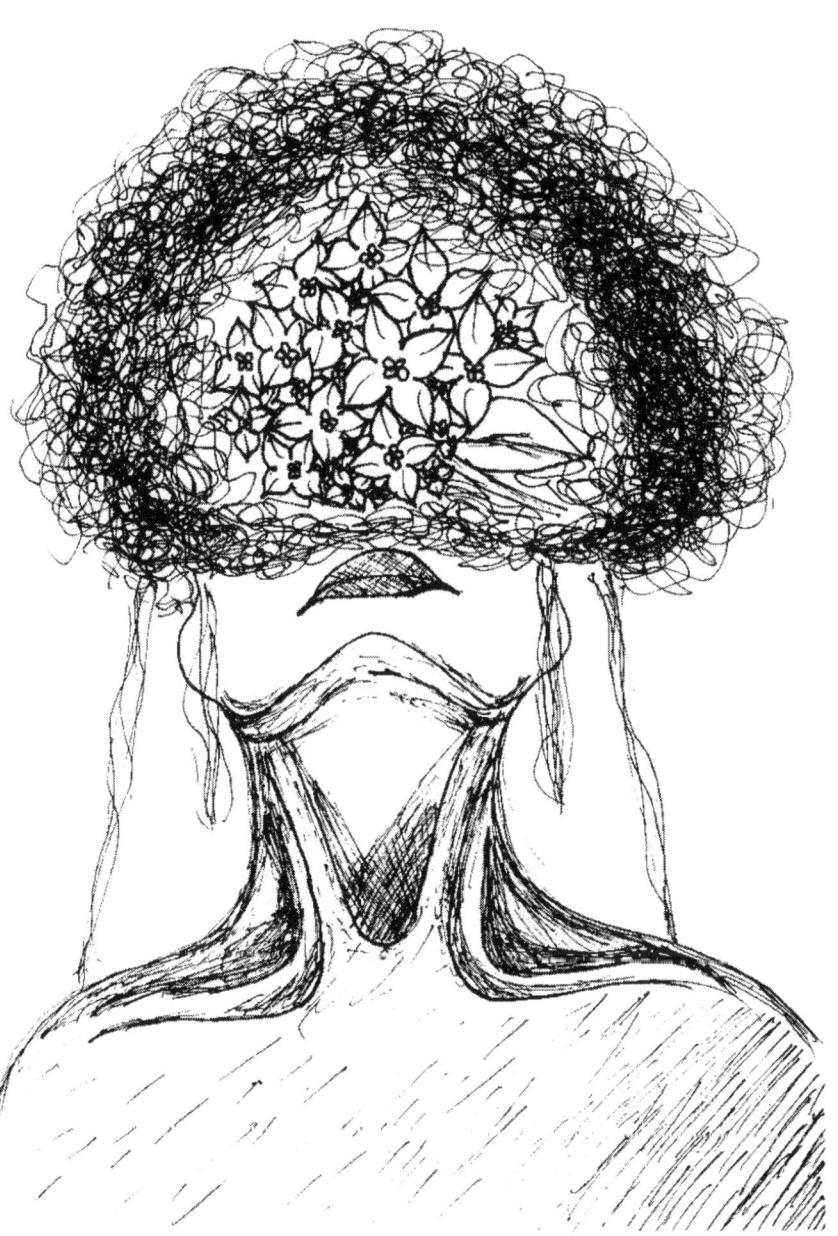

Never allow someone else's

small mindedness

to stop you from

your goals and

your dreams

in life.

Being alone and at peace, will always be better

than being surround by people who have snakes

lying within.

They'll

never want you to do better than them,

always spreading lies of deception and doubt.

Those are the ones that must be let go, forever.

Being happy is hard,

being depressed is even harder.

Somedays,

I don't want to do anything.

If I don't do anything today,

I'll feel even worst tomorrow.

Sometimes in life, you have

to do hard things.

Just so life can be just a little bit better.

lxxxi

Failure will happen,

it's the inevitable.

To succeed,

Persistence is a must.

Once

you learn from your failure,

you will surely succeed.

lxxxiii

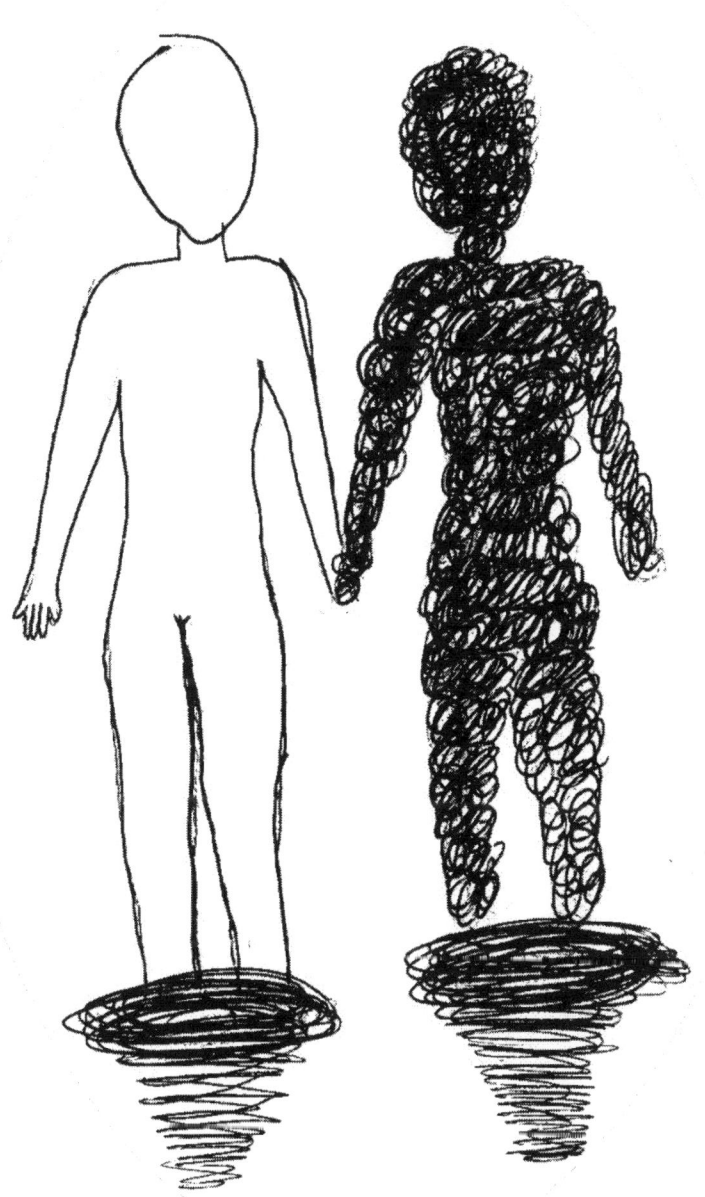

lxxxiv

I have found the person who knows what is best

in life is for you is you.

What people say about you is not who you are.

The only person who knows who you are, is you,

and you alone.

No one else's opinion matters.

Screw societal norms,

be true to yourself and no one else.

lxxxv

Do not let your story be

written by someone else.

Take back control of your narrative.

You are the writer for your story.

So, make it extraordinary, you won't get a second

chance.

lxxxvii

lxxxviii

How do people not see that words are breaking

children to the point of no return.

Why would they not raise a better generation

than the last?

Why not teach children to be kind to everyone.

lxxxix

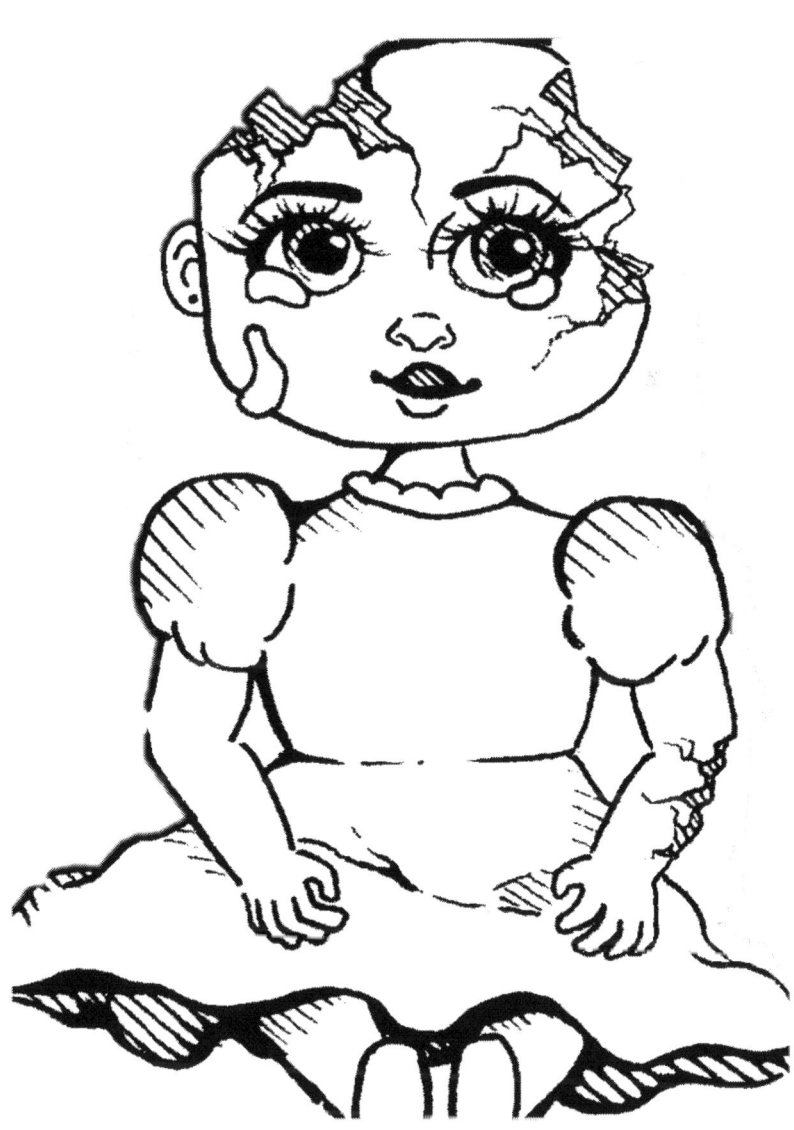

xc

Thanks

for

reading.

xcii

Made in the USA
Middletown, DE
22 December 2022

17373425R00057